PROMISE TO WAIT

MANMOHAN MISHRA

Made with ♥ on the Notion Press Platform
www.notionpress.com

To the kindred spirits who find their voice in the whisper of words, This collection is for those who dare to explore the depths of human emotion and weave stories from the fragments of the heart. To the writers who fill pages with dreams, doubts, and desires—may these poems resonate with your journey. To every poet, storyteller, and dreamer who believes in the healing power of verse, which turns life's fleeting moments into lasting art—this is for you. And to Manmohan Mishra, whose eloquence and heartfelt reflections serve as a testament to the transformative magic of words—thank you for inspiring us to see the extraordinary in the everyday. May these poems remind us of the courage it takes to write, feel, and live authentically. With admiration and gratitude,

[Manmohan Mishra]

Contents

Foreword *vii*

Preface *ix*

Acknowledgements *xi*

Prologue *xiii*

1. Life's Letter 1
2. Finding Paths 3
3. Becoming You 6
4. For You 8
5. Eternal Echoes 10
6. Heart's Memory 12
7. Limitless Love 14
8. Deep Love 16
9. Today's Canvas 18
10. Always Here 20
11. My Calm 22
12. Heart Remembers 24
13. Soft Whispers 26
14. You Matter 28
15. Silent Peace 31
16. Lingering Song 33
17. Silent Weight 35
18. Guiding Light 37
19. Empty Days 39
20. Quiet Yearning 41

Contents

21. Silent Scream 43

22. Love's Whisper 44

23. Radiant Smile 46

24. Unwritten Story 48

25. Soul's Craving 50

26. Always You 52

27. Shared Journeys 54

28. Life's Meaning 57

29. Silent Beauty 59

30. Hidden Truths 61

Special Thanks 63

ABOUT THE AUTHOR 65

Foreword

Poetry is a timeless expression, an art that captures the ineffable truths of life, love, and the human spirit. In this heartfelt collection, **Manmohan Mishra** takes us on an introspective journey through the intricate emotions that define our existence. Each poem unfolds like a whispered conversation between the writer and the reader, bringing to life themes of yearning, gratitude, growth, and resilience.

Mishra's words resonate deeply, not because they seek grandeur, but because they reflect the authentic struggles and triumphs we all carry. The verses are rich with imagery, layered with meaning, and steeped in tenderness. Whether invoking the pain of love lost, the hope of self-renewal, or the quiet beauty of ordinary moments, Mishra's poetry speaks to the universal experiences of the heart.

This collection is not just a compilation of poems—it is a celebration of humanity in all its contradictions. Vulnerability becomes a strength; pain transforms into wisdom; and longing gives way to the courage to dream again. Mishra invites readers to find solace and strength in these pages, to recognize fragments of their own lives in his lines, and to carry these reflections into their everyday world.

For those fortunate enough to hold this book, prepare to feel deeply. These poems will comfort you in your solitude, challenge you to see beauty in imperfection, and inspire you to embrace both the sorrow and joy of life. **Manmohan Mishra's** poetry is a gift of perspective—a reminder that even in the quietest corners of our lives, there is always room for love, growth, and light.

Preface

Writing these poems has been a deeply personal journey, allowing me to articulate emotions that often go unspoken. Poetry has always been my medium of reflection—a way to capture the fleeting whispers of joy, love, longing, and resilience. The words here stem from a place of vulnerability and connection, where life's intricate moments find their voice.

This collection began as scattered thoughts during quiet moments—some inspired by nature, others by relationships that shaped me, and some by the universal quest for meaning. Over time, these fragments wove together into themes of hope, transformation, and human beauty. Each piece reflects my experiences and the emotions we share, creating a bridge between the personal and the universal.

I wrote these verses not as a final statement but as an invitation to pause and feel. They are meant to resonate with those who have faced life's storms and celebrated its bright skies. Whether it's finding solace in dawn's quiet, embracing individuality, or navigating the labyrinth of love, I hope these poems stir something within you, as they did for me.

Thank you for allowing me to share my world through these pages. May these poems serve as a reminder that every journey, no matter how winding, holds a story worth telling.

Acknowledgements

In the symphony of emotions captured within "Promise To Wait" I extend heartfelt gratitude to those who inspire and breathe life into these verses. Your presence in my journey has made this collection a meaningful reflection of love, life, and philosophy. Thank you for being part of the book.

I would like to express my appreciation to all those who have inspired me along the way, including[Amritanjali Mishra, Murli Manohar Mishra, Tetra Devi, Rakesh Kumar Mishra, Kiran Mishra, Rajesh Mishra, Rajnikant Mishra, Animesh Anand, Animesh Sharma, Vandevi Mishra, Jasmita Chaudhary, Anjali Gaikwad] Thank you for your support.

Prologue

Life is filled with moments that touch our hearts and shape who we are. This book of poetry is a collection of those moments—feelings of love, loss, joy, and hope. Each poem is like a conversation with the soul, offering comfort, reflection, and a reminder of what it means to live fully.

These poems are about finding beauty in the small things, strength in tough times, and love in unexpected places. They speak of the light and darkness we all face, inviting you to pause and feel deeply.

Think of this prelude as a gentle introduction, guiding you into the words ahead. These poems don't tell just one story—they tell many. As you read, you might even find pieces of your own heart in their lines.

1. Life's Letter

I want you to wake with the dawn's warm kiss,
To greet each new day with a heart full of bliss.
Feel gratitude rise like the sun in the sky,
Inviting you gently to spread your wings and fly.
Imagine the energy flowing within,
A wellspring of dreams waiting to begin.
Release all your fears, let them fade like the mist,
See the unknown as a puzzle, waiting to be kissed.
You hold all the pieces, each one is your own,
Building a future that's brightly your own.
Don't let doubt linger, don't dwell on regret,
For the strength that you seek is yours to beget.
Start with a whisper, take small, steady steps,
With each little victory, the world gently preps.
The past is a lesson, not a chain to confine,
Let go of what binds you, let your spirit align.
You are the creator of dreams yet untold,
With belief as your guide, let your journey unfold.
You don't need permission; trust in your spark,
For the light that you carry can illuminate the dark.
So rise with intention, let your heart lead the way,
Embrace every moment, let joy have its say.
In love with your life, let each chapter surprise,

For you are the story, and it's yours to realize.

2. Finding Paths

This world is a challenge, living's never light,
Each step can be heavy, but that's part of the fight.
No one will arrive with solutions in hand;
It's up to you to rise, to take a stand.
Use your time wisely; let it not slip away,
Create memories, learn, let mistakes lead the way.
Stumble and falter, but always stand tall,
Your strength is your guide, through it all.
When life feels misaligned and you start to stray,
Pause for a moment, take a breath, find your way.
Tidy your thoughts, sip some coffee, reset,
Each lesson you learn is a gift, don't forget.
Storms may sweep in, but they'll pass with the night,
You have the power to make your path bright.
With each new day comes a chance to explore,
Chase what brings joy, let your spirit soar.
Travel far and wide, let love be your guide,
Be humble and open; embrace every ride.
Engage in what sparks your heart and your soul,
Every moment counts; let your passions take hold.
This life is your canvas—paint it with care,
Be bold and be true in all that you dare.
Don't fret about tomorrow; let the past drift away,

Live fully and freely, make the most of today.
Know yourself deeply; let your true self unfold,
Accept your own journey, both timid and bold.
Work hard and be kind, let simplicity reign,
Find beauty in moments, even in pain.
Each person you meet has their own silent fight,
Choose kindness and warmth; let love be your light.
Fear may be present, but you hold the key,
Face what you fear; let your spirit be free.
People may wound you, but don't close off your heart,
Love again bravely; each end is a start.
Friendship is a treasure that brightens the way,
In laughter and sorrow, they're here to stay.
Life teaches us lessons in joy and in strife,
Each moment you cherish brings depth to your life.
Release the burdens that keep you confined,
Time heals all wounds; let resilience unwind.
Stand up for your values, be strong in your voice,
Help those who need it; let kindness be your choice.
Remember your blessings and share what you can,
Speak your truth boldly, as only you can.
So reach for the stars, let your dreams take flight,
Be a daydreamer, a night thinker, embrace the light.
Life's meant for expression, not just to impress,
Give every day the chance to be your best.
Stay curious, stay brave, let your heart lead the way,
Life's a grand adventure; join in the play.

This journey is yours; let your spirit arise,
In each precious moment, let love be your prize.

3. Becoming You

I want you to transform, to rise and to grow,
To be different from now, let your true self show.
Aspire to be better, but not in comparison's name,
Forge your own path, ignite your own flame.
Mold your own shape, let your spirit take flight,
Avoid the same patterns that dim your inner light.
Aim toward horizons that your heart yearns to seek,
Not just the trails where your friends dare to peek.
Embrace your setbacks, let them teach you anew,
Fear not the missteps that once troubled you.
See the same dreams I cherish, yet from your own view,
Find your unique vantage, let your vision be true.
I long to recognize you, yet crave something rare,
A reflection not mirrored, but vibrant and fair.
You'll carry humility, yet stand tall and proud,
Weathering pressures, not lost in the crowd.
You'll thrive in your rhythm, in your own sacred race,
Victory won't matter if it's just for the chase.
I'll see you in moments beyond what is near,
In a future unfolding, where your path will be clear.
Exceed all the dreams that once filled my mind,
But hold onto the roots that you'll always find.
For I am your whisper, the echo in you,

The voice of encouragement in all that you do.
So embrace who you are, and let your heart soar,
Be the one you envision, and always seek more.
In this journey of life, let your spirit ignite,
Be different, be you—shine your own light.

4. For You

Here are the words I wish to share,
I want you to be happy, wrapped in love's warm air.
May someone else feel the light of your smile,
And know the joy I found in your presence for a while.
I hope you remember the laughter we shared,
Even though you hurt me, I know you cared.
What we had, was it love? I'm not sure,
But losing you taught me I could endure.
Your fingers on my lips, the secrets we spun,
You confided in me like I was the only one.
I've kept your whispers safe, treasures I hold,
A bond forged in trust, more precious than gold.
I'm sorry for pushing you when I meant to draw near,
If I felt like home, it was you who made it clear.
You were my refuge, a safe place to land,
In the chaos of life, you held my hand.
I love you fiercely, with a depth hard to explain,
Ready to fight for you, through joy and through pain.
I miss you profoundly, no matter the miles,
In every heartbeat, I carry your smiles.
You made me feel human, alive in the fray,
Your touch was a spark that lit up my way.
When shadows closed in and hope felt so small,

You showed me the strength I had hidden in thrall.
In the time we were close, you filled me with light,
Galaxies thrummed in my veins, stars danced in my sight.
I'm grateful to fate for the moments we shared,
Yet I ache for the loss, a love unprepared.
There are countless things I long to convey,
This is my solace, my heart on display.
You may never read this, but it eases my soul,
To articulate feelings, to let the words roll.
Thank you for showing me how love could feel,
For the warmth and the wonder, the moments so real.
You stood by my side through the storms that we faced,
And your presence remains in every space.
I remember our first text, how my heart raced,
Late nights turned to dawn, in every word I was laced.
You gave me a story worth holding on tight,
For the beauty of us, I'll forever hold light.

5. Eternal Echoes

The clock whispers one-thirty-nine,
Thoughts of you linger like the sweetest wine.
In every heartbeat, your essence I find,
Missing you deeply, yet grateful in kind.
When I ache for your presence, it reminds me of bliss,
That love, irrevocable, exists in this miss.
My sweet mermaid, with a soul intertwined,
You're the last thought I cradle as I drift into night.
I think of you waking, the dawn in your eyes,
And how your laughter can light up the skies.
Thank you for allowing me into your grace,
I cherish this privilege; it's my heart's rightful place.
I want you to flourish, to shine with delight,
To feel so accomplished, your cheeks warmed by light.
Share with me stories of burdens you bear,
The moments that thrill you, the joys that you share.
Yet here in the quiet, I ponder and sigh,
Could we have worked if the stars were aligned?
If we met in a season where hearts weren't so torn,
I feel you were made for me, a love reborn.
You carved your initials into my tender heart,
Tattooed in ink, you were my every part.
From beginning to end, I thought we were whole,

Now I grapple with shadows that dance in my soul.
I wrestle with blame, with the roles we both played,
Was I too clingy, or perhaps too afraid?
Did I let others dictate the love that I knew,
While all the while, I just wanted you?
You're not the villain; you're an angel divine,
Sent to mend pieces of this heart, once confined.
What do you do when perfection brings pain?
When neither of us wanted the love to wane?
So here I stand, with memories that shine,
Of laughter and whispers, your hand in mine.
Though distance now stretches between us like sea,
Know that you're cherished, you're part of me.
I love you, my darling, in ways that feel true,
Through heartache and longing, my heart beats for you.
May you always find joy, may your spirit be free,
For in this vast universe, you're forever with me.

6. Heart's Memory

I still remember the moment we first called,
The voice recordings, the texts—I can't recall.
No regrets in the journey, just sorrow in the seams,
For every time we parted, it tore at my dreams.
Deep down, I know love lingers like a song,
Yet seeing you leave feels profoundly wrong.
I search for your essence in others I find,
But none can replace what you left behind.
I miss how you smiled, the warmth of your gaze,
The way you made me feel, like I was ablaze.
I'm sorry for moments I brought you dismay,
For all the confusion that led us astray.
For you, I wish happiness, a love that feels true,
A shelter from storms, a safe space for you.
When tears fill your eyes, know I'm right by your side,
I'll hold you through darkness, in love, we confide.
I love you at your best, I cherish your worst,
In a world of uncertainties, you quench my thirst.
Our story is magic, a tale yet untold,
A bond that's extraordinary, more precious than gold.
You are not just my world; you're my everything,
With you, I've found solace, the joy that you bring.
I'm here for the long haul, through thick and through thin,

With you, I have hope, where love can begin.
I love you for the depths that you see in my soul,
For the strength you inspire, for making me whole.
You glimpse the best me, beyond all the strife,
A connection that transcends the trials of life.
How lucky I am to share this gift of you,
Knowing our paths will cross in the lives that are due.
In every crowded room, I'll search for your face,
For the joy in our laughter, in our sacred space.
Until we unite, know this truth I impart:
You have a special spot, forever in my heart.
Through every goodbye, and each tear that we shed,
I'll carry your love, where dreams have been bred.
So here's to our journey, wherever it leads,
To love that is timeless, to planting new seeds.
I'll wait for you always, in the shadows, the light,
You're always with me, in both day and night.

7. Limitless Love

I want all of you—each moment, each day,
To share laughter in the kitchen, as we dance and play.
Fingers tangled in your hair, your warmth close to mine,
Whispers and sweet kisses, lost in a world so fine.
As we weave stories in bed, with voices bright and bold,
Every giggle and shared secret becomes a treasure to hold.
From cookies to cozy nights, let's fill our hearts with cheer,
In a clean, warm home, where love conquers fear.
Picture us on that swing, gently swaying under the sun,
Creating our own tales, where two souls become one.
I'll leave you little notes, tokens of my affection,
Reminders of my love, a deep and lasting connection.
You may not know the depth of what you mean to me,
How your voice echoes softly, like waves in the sea.
In quiet moments, I think of you, both day and night,
Your laughter is my comfort, your presence my light.
Everything about you captivates my heart so true,
From the way your smile glimmers to the way you imbue
Magic into the mundane, turning every touch into delight,
With you, my world is vivid, painted in love's light.
My love for you is timeless, an endless, flowing stream,
A bond that deepens daily, woven through every dream.
In every glance, I see our past and future entwined,

A love story unfolding, beautifully aligned.
When we finally embrace on that long-awaited day,
I'll feel my heart expand, as I cherish our way.
Through every high and low, I'll stand faithfully by,
With you, my dear, I've found my reason why.
So here's my promise, heartfelt and true,
To love you deeply in all that we do.
You are my everything, my safe, loving space,
Together we'll navigate life's beautiful race.

8. Deep Love

I miss you more than words can weave,
A tapestry of longing, a heart that can't believe.
Your voice, a melody that dances through my mind,
Your laughter, a symphony, so gentle and so kind.
Those oceanic eyes, they haunt my dreams at night,
A beautiful reminder of love's radiant light.
I crave the warmth of your embrace,
The sweet solace found in your familiar space.
In a crowded room, our silent exchanges say it all,
A look, a fleeting smile, a catch before the fall.
I long for the moments yet to be,
The spontaneous dance parties, just you and me.
Imagining us tangled in laughter, carefree and bold,
Sharing secrets over sandwiches, stories yet untold.
The scent of candles flickering, casting soft, warm glow,
Kissing you softly, wherever we choose to go.
I dream of waking to the peace of your face,
Rolling over, finding you in our cozy place.
Back hugs while brushing teeth, the joy in little things,
Finding magic in the mundane, the love that truly sings.
My heart, can it be mine when you inhabit it whole?
Every thought, every beat, you're woven into my soul.
I cherish those moments, the softness of your touch,

The warmth that envelops me, oh, I miss you so much.
I imagine your hand on my leg, our fingers entwined,
Snuggling before sleep, with laughter redefined.
Watching you peacefully, knowing you're free from strife,
In those precious moments, I find the essence of life.
I want you to know how grateful I truly feel,
For every smile you give me, for every love that's real.
I promise to appreciate you, in all that you do,
For you are my heart, my soulmate—my forever, my you.
So here's to the memories, both now and yet to come,
To the laughter, the love, the joy that makes us one.
In every heartbeat, in every sigh, you're my greatest truth,
In the echoes of my longing, I'll always love you.

9. Today's Canvas

I want you to feel the dawn's embrace,
To wake each morning, bathed in grace,
With gratitude woven in the light,
As the sun spills gold, chasing away the night.
Imagine the energy coursing through your veins,
Like a river unbound, shedding its chains,
Each moment a chance, each heartbeat a song,
In the tapestry of life, where you truly belong.
Do not fear the shadows of the unknown,
See them as puzzles, waiting to be grown.
A labyrinth of dreams, whispering your name,
You hold the pieces, you're the one to claim.
Picture the life you dare to envision,
A masterpiece crafted with heart and precision,
Look back one day, and let wonder arise,
At the journey you took, at the heights you'll realize.
Don't let the whispers of doubt fill your mind,
For within you is strength, unique and kind.
Begin with small steps, let your spirit unfold,
In the softness of moments, be brave and be bold.
Release the strings of what once held you tight,
Embrace every heartbeat, let go of the night.
It's a dance, a journey, not a race to the end,

And in every misstep, new lessons to blend.
Remember, dear heart, you need not a crowd,
To chase after dreams, to stand fierce and proud.
Believe in the magic that flickers within,
You deserve to soar, to lose and to win.
So paint your canvas, brush it with light,
Each stroke a reminder, each color a flight.
You are the artist, the dreamer, the key,
Unlocking the life that's waiting for thee.

10. Always Here

"I love you" is a gentle embrace,
A promise to hold your heart in this space.
It's knowing you whole, without need to change,
Accepting the flaws, the wild and the strange.
It means I'm with you in shadows and light,
In moments of laughter and long, quiet nights.
Through storms of your mood, and the weight of the day,
I stand by your side, come what may.
I'll cherish your secrets, the whispers you share,
With no judgment to weigh, just an open heart's care.
In this bond that we build, through struggles we face,
I'll fight for our love, for this beautiful place.
When doubts swirl and spin, and the world feels too loud,
Know my love for you stands fierce and proud.
It doesn't waver on days that feel tough;
I'm here, my darling, even when life gets rough.
I long for the evenings, our books side by side,
Where comfort wraps round us, and peace is our guide.
With puzzles and laughter, with dreams to ignite,
In the softness of dusk, I crave your light.
Face paint Fridays, with giggles and cheer,
Transforming our moments, as we draw ever near.
I want to witness you, in all that you do,

In your joy and your struggles, I'm here just for you.
To see you create, to watch dreams take flight,
To cherish each moment, from morning till night.
Your smile, your laughter, the spark in your eyes,
Is the magic I treasure, the sweetest surprise.
I love you, my dear, in all that you are,
Through the highs and the lows, you're my guiding star.
Always, in all ways, my heart is your home,
Together, my love, we'll never be alone.

11. My Calm

It's you, the anchor in my stormy sea,
The one I rush to after a long day's plea.
In the quiet hours when the world's asleep,
You're the warmth beside me, the love that I keep.
You're the reason for laughter in midnight's glow,
The joy in my heart that continues to grow.
Late-night drives just to savor the night,
Chasing the stars, everything feels right.
With you, I crave those simple delights,
Candlelit dinners, and movie nights.
Morning whispers over coffee, sweet and warm,
In every moment shared, you're my calm.
Adventures await, with hands intertwined,
Exploring the world, two souls aligned.
From lakeside strolls to hikes through the trees,
Every step together feels like a breeze.
Let's build a fort, escape to our dreams,
Wrapped in each other, or so it seems.
Through laughter and tears, through joy and strife,
You're the one I choose for this beautiful life.
When challenges rise and the shadows descend,
I'll be your support, your partner, your friend.
In every heartbeat, through all that we face,

It's you that I cherish, my heart's sacred place.
So here's my truth, as clear as can be,
In this journey together, it's you and me.
No doubts in my mind, just a love that is true,
Forever and always, it's simply you.

12. Heart Remembers

Speak to me, my love, in whispers soft and true,
For in this silence, all I feel is you.
A longing that trembles, a pulse deep inside,
I miss you fiercely, my heart open wide.
It aches to see you unrecognized, unseen,
You deserve the world, to feel like a queen.
Adored and uplifted, your spirit embraced,
In a dance of support, where love is interlaced.
Life can be tangled, a maze of despair,
But know that my faith in you is always there.
I want you to thrive, to find joy in your days,
To feel fulfilled in your own unique ways.
You are worthy, my dear, for all that you are,
Not bound by your work or a measure of stars.
Your essence alone makes you precious to me,
A treasure more radiant than eyes can see.
When I say "I love you," it's more than a phrase,
It carries my heart through all of life's maze.
In every syllable, my soul finds its song,
A promise to cherish, to hold you lifelong.
Through every struggle, each off-kilter day,
I'll choose you again, come what may.
You've pulled me from shadows, taught me what's real,

In your arms, I've learned how true love can heal.
So whenever you're searching, just look at me,
As your brightest star, shining endlessly.
I'm the laughter that dances, the warmth of the sun,
A reminder, my darling, that you are the one.
My love, vast and boundless, transcends every time,
Echoes of my heart, forever entwined.

13. Soft Whispers

I wish I could speak to you, to bridge this divide,
To share the weight of feelings I can't seem to hide.
Today feels heavy, like a storm in my chest,
Missing you deeply, longing for rest.
The drive was a journey through thoughts that won't cease,
Each mile a reminder, searching for peace.
Overwhelmed by emotions that twist and collide,
I try to embrace them, though it's hard to confide.
In the warmth of my family, I find fleeting delight,
But as night draws closer, my heart takes flight.
Tears fall like raindrops, I'm not sure why,
Just a rush of sensations, a quiet goodbye.
It's a mix of the mundane, the worries I hold,
The weight of the world can feel heavy and cold.
I know it's okay to feel anxious and small,
But I wish I could soften the edge of it all.
I think of you often, and the days that feel long,
Frustration and hope dance, a bittersweet song.
But I don't want to linger in shadows of doubt,
I simply want you to know what I'm about.
You are so beautiful, in every single way,
Through highs and through lows, in the light and the gray.
So hear this, my love, in the silence of night:

I carry you with me, you're my heart's guiding light.

14. You Matter

I want more of you, a truth I can't disguise,
Every moment spent with you lights up my skies.
If I'm honest, I yearn for all that you are,
To take care of you, my beautiful star.
You deserve to be cherished, adored every day,
In my heart, you'll forever hold sway.
Right now, tears fall, and I'm feeling so raw,
But beneath the sorrow, hope flickers, a law.
It's strange how this feeling connects us somehow,
With my dad's spirit guiding, I sense it right now.
Everything aligns in a cosmic ballet,
Fireworks of love, illuminating our way.
As we stand on the brink of a future unknown,
I feel an electric pulse, in every love tone.
The safety I find in your gaze is profound,
A connection unbroken, where true love is found.
Healing together, both you and I,
In your arms, my worries begin to fly.
I want to keep you, to hold you so tight,
To build a life filled with laughter and light.
Every smile that graces your lips makes me glow,
I'm here to create joy, to help you know.
I want to "kiss" you when the moment feels right,

To spoil you with love, to make your heart bright.
You deserve the moon and all that it brings,
Since I'm your moon, I'll gather the stars' wings.
Every glimmer reflects the strength you possess,
You've fought so hard, love, through each little stress.
This is your time; it's time to receive,
The goodness you've sown, now starting to weave.
Proud of you, darling, I wish we could cheer,
Celebrate your journey, hold you near.
You've given so much, and now it's your turn,
To bask in the light and feel your heart burn.
You're destined for greatness, a truth I can see,
Keep shining your light; let your spirit fly free.
Some days, I can't grasp that this love is for real,
A dream that envelops, a heart that can feel.
I thought love was static, just a pass or a fail,
But with you, it blossoms, a grand, endless trail.
You make my heart race, with every sweet glance,
In your presence, I find my soul's gentle dance.
I can't stop thinking about you, day and night,
You've woven yourself in, and it feels so right.
If you asked for chicken fingers every single night,
I'd serve them with joy, make everything bright.
From the last of my starburst to music on trips,
Every small act a treasure, our love on my lips.
Your cheeks hold a softness, your smile draws me near,
I want to kiss you there, my love, oh so dear.

To snuggle close, listen to your heart's gentle beat,
To feel your breath rise, to savor the sweet.
Watching you relax in the warmth of my hold,
In those quiet moments, our love story unfolds.
Tonight, I'm in my feels, and it's beautifully right,
A pull towards you, a beacon of light.
I want to drive to you, to bridge every space,
To wrap you in arms, to lose myself in your grace.
Looking into your eyes, I'll find home once more,
With every embrace, I'll keep coming back for.
I want to feel that spark, the electricity fly,
To taste every moment, to breathe you, oh my.
With whispers of love that dance in the air,
I'll pull you in closer, dispelling each care.
I love you so deeply, with all that I am,
In every heartbeat, it's you I'll always claim.
So here's my promise, forever to hold,
To treasure you, love, in this story we've told.
With each passing day, my heart's open wide,
I want more of you always, with you by my side.

15. Silent Peace

My heart feels heavy, like a weight on my chest,
Imagining your sad eyes, longing for rest.
If only I could be there, to hold you so tight,
To wrap you in warmth, to be your light.
I want to comfort you, to wipe away tears,
To celebrate your victories, to calm all your fears.
You're soaring high, my love, believe in your grace,
Allow yourself joy in the things that are true.
You've faced so much, yet you stand so tall,
I see your strength shining; it's a beautiful call.
In the quiet moments, I wish you could feel,
The love that surrounds you, so steady and real.
It's okay to feel heavy; it's okay to be sad,
You've carried so much, my beautiful lad.
Part of me wants to hold you, to soothe your tired soul,
To remind you of strength, to help you feel whole.
You've battled through storms, and I'm here by your side,
To cheer you on fiercely, with love as our guide.
Rest, my dear heart, let the world fade away,
You've earned every moment, let yourself play.
I wish I could be there, to hold your soft hand,
To bring you sweet comfort, to help you withstand.
I'd rub your weary neck, play with your hair,

Creating a sanctuary, a space we can share.
I love you so deeply; I miss your sweet light,
Your laughter, your freckles, that make everything bright.
You're a beacon of hope, a light in my dark,
With you by my side, I'm ignited, I spark.
So let your tears flow; they're a part of the ride,
But know, my love, I'm always right by your side.
Together we'll journey through shadows and sun,
In the rhythm of love, we'll conquer, we'll run.
You're a miracle, darling, in every way,
And I'm forever grateful for you, come what may.

16. Lingering Song

I miss you more than words can weave,
A tapestry of longing, a heart that can't believe.
Your voice, a melody that dances through my mind,
Your laughter, a symphony, so gentle and so kind.
Those oceanic eyes, they haunt my dreams at night,
A beautiful reminder of love's radiant light.
I crave the warmth of your embrace,
The sweet solace found in your familiar space.
In a crowded room, our silent exchanges say it all,
A look, a fleeting smile, a catch before the fall.
I long for the moments yet to be,
The spontaneous dance parties, just you and me.
Imagining us tangled in laughter, carefree and bold,
Sharing secrets over sandwiches, stories yet untold.
The scent of candles flickering, casting soft, warm glow,
Kissing you softly, wherever we choose to go.
I dream of waking to the peace of your face,
Rolling over, finding you in our cozy place.
Back hugs while brushing teeth, the joy in little things,
Finding magic in the mundane, the love that truly sings.
My heart, can it be mine when you inhabit it whole?
Every thought, every beat, you're woven into my soul.
I cherish those moments, the softness of your touch,

The warmth that envelops me, oh, I miss you so much.
I imagine your hand on my leg, our fingers entwined,
Snuggling before sleep, with laughter redefined.
Watching you peacefully, knowing you're free from strife,
In those precious moments, I find the essence of life.
I want you to know how grateful I truly feel,
For every smile you give me, for every love that's real.
I promise to appreciate you, in all that you do,
For you are my heart, my soulmate—my forever, my you.
So here's to the memories, both now and yet to come,
To the laughter, the love, the joy that makes us one.
In every heartbeat, in every sigh, you're my greatest truth,
In the echoes of my longing, I'll always love you.

17. Silent Weight

I wish you knew how hard it can be,
Not to text you when you're on my mind constantly.
Every moment that passes, my heart feels tight,
Wanting to reach out, to share my night.
It's tough to stay busy, to push thoughts away,
But in the silence, it's you I think of each day.
Do you see the struggle, the feelings I hide?
How hard it is not to let love be my guide?
I love you more than I can ever say,
But fear holds me back, pushing you away.
Forgive me if I care too much, it's true,
Every thought and heartbeat just lead me to you.
I'm sorry for sharing my little dramas and strife,
When you have your own battles, your own life.
But deep down, I wish you could see,
How much I long for you to want me.
I know I'm not easy, I worry and doubt,
Sometimes I overreact and feel left out.
But when I love, I do it with all my heart,
A promise to cherish, never to part.
If I love you, I love you strong and bold,
With warmth so bright, it can never grow cold.
You'll find in my heart, a safe place to stay,

With someone who cares, who won't walk away.
I may not be perfect; I stumble and fall,
But in loving you deeply, I give you my all.
You've shown me what love is, real and clear,
And in your warm presence, I feel no fear.
Every time we're together, my heart takes flight,
Butterflies dancing, my smile shining bright.
You help me come out from the shell that I've made,
In your gentle embrace, all my worries fade.
I love your quirks, your kindness, your grace,
Your laughter, your clumsiness, every trace.
When you're playful and free, it lights up my day,
It shows me you trust me in your own special way.
And as I look into those beautiful eyes,
I see a future with you, a wonderful prize.
I'm serious when I say, my heart is your own,
In the story of my life, with you, I have grown.
So know that forever, in all that we do,
My love will be steady, always true.
You are my dream, my guide, my light,
Together we'll shine, through day and through night

18. Guiding Light

Let me begin with a whispered prayer,
For fate that brought you to my side,
In shadows deep, where hope felt rare,
You became my beacon, my guiding light.
When life was shrouded in doubt and despair,
You stepped in, transforming the night,
With every smile, you filled the air,
A warmth that made my spirit take flight.
I've never known a love so true,
Like a compass pointing straight to you,
You've shown me the beauty in every day,
A melody sweet that guides my way.
In your laughter, I find my joy,
In your eyes, my dreams unfold,
With every moment, you make me feel,
A love so deep, a bond so bold.
I vow to lift you, to help you soar,
To stand beside you, to be your core,
For you deserve all the stars in the sky,
With you, my love, I long to fly.
Your light has brightened my darkest days,
With you, I've learned to dance and play,
You've taught me what it means to care,

To celebrate every moment we share.
Without you, my world feels incomplete,
A puzzle missing its crucial piece,
But when you're near, I feel so whole,
You are my fire, my heart, my soul.
In every heartbeat, in every sigh,
I promise to love you, to never say goodbye,
Through trials and joys, I'll stand by your side,
With you, my love, there's nothing to hide.
Each day I'm grateful, each night I dream,
Of all the moments that make us a team,
You are my partner, my confidant, my friend,
Together, my love, we'll rise and transcend.
So here's my heart, my hand, my all,
I'll catch you whenever you feel small,
With each passing second, my love will grow,
For you, my dear, are the light I know.
In the quiet moments, in laughter and tears,
I'll cherish you always, through all of our years,
For with every breath, with all that I am,
I love you completely, and that's my plan.
So let's weave our dreams, let's chase the sun,
Together, my love, we'll forever run,
Through storms and through calm, in shadows and light,
You are my everything, my heart's pure delight.

19. Empty Days

I miss you like the moon craves the sun's warm touch,
In the stillness of night, your light calls to me,
A gentle whisper through the shadows,
Reminding me of what it means to truly be.
Your presence lingers, like a soft, golden hue,
Painting my world with colors so bright,
You nurture the garden of my heart,
Turning barren moments into vibrant delight.
Each day without you feels like a faded dream,
A canvas stripped of all its brilliant shades,
But your love, like sunlight, breaks through the seams,
Revealing the beauty in the serenade it makes.
You're the strength in my roots, the fire in my soul,
With you, I blossom, reaching ever higher,
Even when the soil feels rough and unkind,
Your warmth ignites my inner desire.
So shine, my love, let your brilliance flow,
Illuminate the paths we've yet to explore,
For in your glow, I've learned to grow,
In your embrace, I find what I adore.
Tears of joy fall freely, a testament of grace,
You've transformed my heart with every tender glance,
I celebrate the journey, the love we embrace,

In this dance of life, we'll forever take a chance.
Together we'll bloom, like flowers in the sun,
Embracing the colors that love has unfurled,
For you are my favorite, my only one,
The brightest light in my ever-expanding world.
So here's to the moments we're yet to create,
To laughter and whispers, to dreams yet to find,
In every heartbeat, I know it's not too late,
For in our love, we leave the shadows behind.

20. Quiet Yearning

I stand here waiting, heart open wide,
Like a flower yearning for the spring's gentle tide.
I'm the moon in the night, craving the sun's glow,
Lost in the shadows, where soft whispers flow.
Like the river that dreams of a vast, open sea,
I ache for your touch, for your love set me free.
You're the warmth of the sun on a cold winter's day,
Yet I reach for your heart, and it drifts far away.
The earth spins in silence, longing for rain,
Just as my soul aches, caught in this pain.
You're the light in my darkness, the spark in my night,
But the distance between us feels endless, a plight.
Each moment I linger, with hopes that ignite,
But love feels elusive, like stars out of sight.
I search for your laughter, your gaze that inspires,
But it seems like a dream, as my heart quietly tires.
Oh, how I wish for the magic we crave,
For a love that can conquer, that's fierce and that's brave.
Like the dawn that meets dusk in a beautiful blend,
I long for the moment when our souls can transcend.
So here I stand, with my heart in my hands,
Waiting for love that perfectly understands.
With every heartbeat, I whisper your name,

Hoping one day, it won't be the same.
You are my sun, my sea, my beloved shore,
And I'll keep on reaching, forever wanting more.
For in this vast world, with its twists and its bends,
I believe in our love, where the longing finally ends.

21. Silent Scream

The ache in my heart is a silent scream,
A plea for connection that feels miles away.
I watch you slip from my grasp like sand,
Each grain a memory, a broken promise,
Echoes of laughter now whispers of pain.
The pain is unspeakable, a burden too heavy,
Words falter and fade, lost in the air.
Even those closest seem distant, unfocused,
Leaving me stranded, alone with my fears,
As shadows stretch long, and silence ensnares.
Yet, I hold on, a fragile hope flickering,
A candle against winds that threaten to blow,
I wait for the moment you might truly see
The love I cradle in tear-filled eyes,
A beacon of warmth in this cold, empty glow.
So here in the stillness, I whisper your name,
A mantra of longing, a promise to wait.
Though distance may grow, and time may betray,
In the depths of my heart, I will always believe
That love can bridge gaps, that we'll find our way.

22. Love's Whisper

I don't know how to begin this tale of my heart,
But I think I'm in love with you, that's just the start.
Each thought of you blooms like flowers in spring,
In the garden of my soul, it's you who takes wing.
You bring a warmth I've never known,
A feeling of belonging, a place I can call home.
In your laughter, I find a melody sweet,
You make every moment feel beautifully complete.
Through the shadows and light, I want to be there,
For your joyful triumphs, and burdens you bear.
Every single part of you, both your light and your shade,
Is a treasure I cherish, a bond we have made.
In dreams of tomorrow, you fill my heart's view,
A future bright and vibrant, painted with hues.
No one else has shown me this kind of embrace,
In your eyes, I discover my sacred space.
I promise to stand by you, in every rise and fall,
To hold you closer when the world feels too tall.
With gentle reminders of how loved you are,
You shine like the moon, my ever-bright star.
So here's to the mornings when I wake by your side,
To whispers of love, where our hearts coincide.
I send you my warmth, across distance and time,

In the rhythm of our hearts, I know we'll align.
Come rest in my arms, let's dream of the day,
When we'll laugh and dance the night away.
With kisses that linger and joy in our song,
You're my forever, to you I belong.
In each silent moment, know I'm thinking of you,
With every heartbeat, my love feels anew.
I miss you dearly, yet I know it's so clear,
In this beautiful journey, it's you I hold dear.

23. Radiant Smile

In your presence, the world shifts, colors bloom anew,
Each glance a gentle whisper, every laugh a sky so blue.
We slip into a moment where time loses its thread,
Seconds stretch like summer days, when thoughts of you are spread.
When you're away, the clock stands still, a heavy, longing weight,
Minutes drag like shadows, love, as I patiently await.
But when you're near, my heart ignites, burning bright and free,
With you, I find my courage, together, just you and me.
You shine through cloudy mornings, a beacon in the haze,
In the labyrinth of life, you guide me through the maze.
With you, the toughest battles feel lighter than a sigh,
You lift me up, you fill my cup; in your warmth, I can fly.
Your belief in me is magic, a potion strong and rare,
It stirs my soul, awakens dreams, lifting me into the air.
When I first saw your smile, something deep within awoke,
A spark ignited, a promise made, words unspoken but bespoke.
You break the chains of doubt that once held you in despair,
With every step you take, you show the world your care.
For every smile you share, for every moment of grace,

You're a masterpiece unfolding, a light in every space.
You give and give, and yet, your heart remains so pure,
In a world that often overlooks, you make love feel secure.
So here's my vow, my darling, as we journey hand in hand,
I'll treasure every heartbeat, as together we will stand.
You are my joy, my laughter, the dream I long to chase,
In every single moment, I find home in your embrace.
So let's paint our tomorrows with colors bold and bright,
For in this dance of life, it's you who brings the light.

24. Unwritten Story

Where to begin? My heart is full,
In a world of chaos, you're my gentle pull.
Thank you for being my truest light,
For understanding my silence, for making things right.
When joy paints my days, you shine with me,
And when shadows creep in, you help me see.
Your soft words wrap around my fears,
In your embrace, I find solace, my dear.
You're the first thought that greets the dawn,
My favorite person, where my heart belongs.
I don't want to wander too far from your side,
With you, love's journey is a thrilling ride.
"Distance makes us love each other more,"
Each moment apart strengthens the core.
I love you fiercely, more than I've said,
With dreams of forever, we'll forge ahead.
Your laughter is a melody that lingers sweet,
Your smile, a warmth that makes my heart beat.
I cherish your quirks, your gentle ways,
In every shared moment, my spirit sways.
You are my anchor, my laughter, my friend,
The one I lean on, the hand I'll extend.
Together we'll craft memories so bright,

In our little world, everything feels right.
I wish to stay close, to share every dream,
To turn our moments into a beautiful theme.
Even on hard days, I just want your gaze,
To feel your presence in the simplest ways.
Let's weave our story with laughter and cheer,
Creating a tapestry that's beautifully clear.
I want to be the reason you smile and you laugh,
Together we'll navigate this beautiful path.
With love that is deep, unwavering, and true,
Know that forever, my heart belongs to you.
In every heartbeat, in every sigh,
You're my everything, my reason to fly.

25. Soul's Craving

So many thoughts dance in my mind,
Yet words seem to slip, so hard to find.
Where to begin in this vast sea of you,
In your essence, I've found my truest view.
You are the dream I never dared to chase,
Wrapped in warmth, in love's soft embrace.
At just five foot three, with a spark in your gaze,
You light up my life in countless ways.
Your laughter is music, sweet and profound,
A symphony of joy that knows no bound.
In every heartbeat, in every sigh,
With you by my side, I feel I can fly.
When happiness swells, it's you that I see,
And in my darkest hours, it's you who comforts me.
You are my anchor when the storms start to rage,
The calm in my chaos, my favorite page.
You make the mundane feel like a dream,
Every moment with you, more than it seems.
From late-night talks to early morning light,
With you, my love, everything feels right.
You're the one I want after a long, weary day,
The hand I'll hold, come what may.
Whether it's adventures or quiet nights in,

With you, every chapter begins with a grin.
Together we'll build a life full of cheer,
Creating memories, year after year.
You are my laughter, my solace, my friend,
With you by my side, I can always ascend.
So here's my promise, heartfelt and true:
In every moment, I'll cherish you.
You're my forever, my light in the dark,
In this beautiful journey, you've ignited my spark.
So let's walk together, through thick and thin,
With you, my love, I know we'll always win.
You are my treasure, my dream come alive,
I love you more than words can ever describe.

26. Always You

I love you, and I always will,
A truth etched deep, a heart that's still.
You linger in thoughts, like stars in the night,
A warmth in my soul, a guiding light.
Through storms and shadows, you've been my sun,
In every battle fought, you were the one.
I know I faltered, let my hurt take its toll,
But beneath the chaos, it's you who makes me whole.
Memories flood like waves on the shore,
Each laugh and each glance, I cherish even more.
Do you recall those moments, so sweet and so rare?
When time stood still, and we had not a care.
Side by side in a world of our own,
In a crowded room, you felt like home.
Your smile sparked joy, your laughter, my muse,
In the tapestry of life, it's always been you.
Regrets weave shadows in the fabric of time,
What ifs and maybes, they twist in my mind.
If paths had aligned, if the stars had shone bright,
Would we still dance under the soft moonlight?
Though distance may stretch like a river's long bend,
You're woven in dreams that I cannot pretend.
You're the echo of love, the song in my heart,

A bond that remains, even when we're apart.
So here's my confession, as honest as dawn,
You're the one I hold dear, forever my song.
In every heartbeat, in every sigh,
I love you, my darling, and I'll never say goodbye.

27. Shared Journeys

Sometimes, people enter your life,
And you can't foresee the changes they'll bring.
You might not know how deeply they'll touch you,
Or the joy in your heart that they'll gently sing.
If you knew how much they'd mean to you,
Would you act differently when first you met?
A glance, a smile, a spark in the air,
Moments like these, you'll never forget.
Life can feel empty before they arrive,
Then suddenly, everything starts to glow.
With laughter and love, they make you believe,
In a world where your heart can freely flow.
When passion ignites, it feels like a dream,
Like a story that dances in the light.
Every word they say, a melody sweet,
Your heart races fast, everything feels right.
So if you find someone who makes your heart soar,
Hold them close, don't let go, let love be your guide.
Each moment with them is a treasure to keep,
In the warmth of their presence, let your spirits collide.
Don't let chances slip, don't let them fade,
For love like this is precious and rare.
When they're not with you, a piece feels so lost,

Longing for moments you wish you could share.
Memories linger, both joyful and bright,
Life whispers softly in love's gentle tune.
But true love's not perfect; it's a beautiful dance,
Through the storms and the sunshine, you'll both learn and bloom.
People say love is easy, just laughter and light,
But they haven't seen what true love can face.
The strongest bonds grow through trials and tears,
Building a future that time can't erase.
The key is connection, a heart that is true,
Someone who cherishes the real you inside.
At a young age, I found my heart's perfect match,
In their smile, I saw a love I could abide.
Through every season, together we'll stand,
In the laughter, in silence, in joy and in pain.
It's rare to discover someone who feels,
Like home in your heart, your shelter from rain.
You share all your dreams, your hopes and your fears,
They listen with care, wanting to hear more.
In moments of triumph, you celebrate loud,
And in times of sorrow, they're there to restore.
So when you find that one who sees you so clear,
Embrace them with warmth, let your spirits unite.
Cherish each moment, each heartbeat, each sigh,
For love like this is your guiding light.
Here's to the journey, to the love that we make,

To the laughter and tears, every chance that we take.
In the tapestry of life, may our threads intertwine,
Forever together, your heart next to mine.

28. Life's Meaning

In this vast world, you shine so bright,
A rare gem that dances in the light.
Not out of loneliness did my heart take flight,
But in your presence, everything feels right.
You give me strength when I feel small,
A gentle embrace that answers my call.
With every glance, you bring me peace,
A soothing balm that grants my heart release.
The fear of losing you brings me to tears,
A thought so heavy, it shadows my years.
For you are the dream I didn't dare to chase,
A love that wraps me in its warm embrace.
When our eyes meet, the world fades away,
Words become whispers, too shy to stay.
You understand me, deep in your soul,
With you, my love, I feel completely whole.
In your laughter, I find my muse,
A melody that chases away the blues.
You inspire me to leap and to dare,
To chase my dreams without a care.
You pull me closer when I start to sway,
Transforming my chaos into a dance of play.
With every word you speak, I feel the pull,

A gravitational force that makes me full.
Oh, how I cherish the moments we share,
The little things that show how much you care.
From quiet mornings to silly midnight talks,
With you, I'm home, whether we're in crowds or walks.
I want your laughter to fill my days,
Your gentle touch in countless ways.
Your dreams, your hopes, your sweet embrace,
In this journey of life, I want you in every space.
So here's my heart, laid open and true,
In this tapestry of life, it's woven with you.
Together, forever, let's write our own song,
In a love that feels right, where we both belong.

29. Silent Beauty

She walks with grace, a light in her eyes,
A heart so vast, it reaches the skies.
With kindness wrapped in a gentle embrace,
Her laughter, a melody, fills up the space.
She bends for others, a rare, tender heart,
Ready to give, to play her part.
But behind her warmth, a fragility lies,
A past that whispers, a truth that belies.
She carries her stories, though seldom she shares,
A tapestry woven with love and with cares.
Her smile hides battles, fought day after day,
A warrior's spirit, though soft in display.
Cautious and guarded, she stands on her ground,
Yet inside her, a yearning for connection is found.
A desire for laughter, for moments so real,
For someone to see her, someone to feel.
When I first met her, the world seemed to pause,
Her energy drew me, a magnetic cause.
Not for mere pleasure, nor fleeting delight,
But for depth and for truth that ignites the night.
She's more than her past, more than her fears,
A beacon of hope, through laughter and tears.
Those who look closely will find a rare gem,

A loyal companion, a love without end.
So here's to the soul, so vibrant and true,
To the one who gives light, who makes skies so blue.
In her presence, I've learned what it means to be free,
For in her, I've found the best part of me.

30. Hidden Truths

Hold on to this dark embrace,
Let the world fade, find our space.
Cool moonlight drapes the sky,
Whisper dreams as time slips by.
Day's shadows linger, but we'll bend,
Shift the moment, let love ascend.
With you, I've discovered a brand-new part,
No longer lost, you've healed my heart.
This night transforms all that I knew,
In love's reflection, I find the true.
Beneath the stars, a gentle glow,
With every heartbeat, my spirit flows.
I'm calling through every fleeting second,
Whispers of love that time has beckoned.
In every breath, your name I trace,
My thoughts wrapped in your warm embrace.
The air is thick with soft delight,
A melody that stirs the night.
Together we dance, lost in the light,
In your arms, everything feels right.
Hold on to this dark embrace,
As we wander through time and space.
In the coolness, let our spirits glide,

In this moment, forever abide.
With every tick, my heart takes flight,
Calling for you, my guiding light.
Through every second, love rings clear,
In this night's magic, I feel you near.

Special Thanks

Dear all,

I extend my deepest gratitude for the overwhelming support and encouragement I've received from each one of you throughout the journey of writing this book. Your presence in my life has been instrumental in turning my dreams into reality.

First and foremost, I want to express my heartfelt thanks to my late grandparents Tetra Devi and Satyendra Mani Mishra.

Special thanks to my parents, Rajesh Mishra and Vandevi Mishra, who are my pillars of positivity and supportive guides. Your unwavering encouragement and love have been my greatest strength, inspiring me to chase my passion and dreams. You are the driving force behind everything I have achieved.

Murli Manohar Mishra,

Special thanks to my dear elder brother for being my unwavering supporter and constant source of motivation. He has encouraged me to pursue my passion and profession wholeheartedly, and his belief in me has been the driving force behind everything

To my sister, Amritanjali Mishra, you have been my confidant and a constant source of motivation. Thank you for pushing me to be the best version of myself. Without you, the universe feels empty. Thank you for always being there.

Anjali Gaikwad

I want to express my heartfelt gratitude to Anjali Gaikwad, the best person. Thank you for your unwavering support and care during my toughest days. Your presence has been a source of comfort and strength for me.

Animesh Anand,

With your wonderful personality and exceptional teaching skills, you've been a source of motivation and inspiration for me since the beginning. I look up to you for guidance.

My Big Uncle Rakesh Kumar Mishra,

Your unique insights and perspective have enlightened my view of the world. Thank you for sharing your thoughts and time with me. Your impact on my life is significant, and I am grateful for your support.

Once again, thank you all for being an integral part of my journey and for supporting me wholeheartedly. Your love, guidance, and encouragement mean the world to me.

With deep gratitude,

Manmohan Mishra

About The Author

Manmohan Mishra

Hello, and thank you for considering my book. I'm Manmohan Mishra, a full-time engineer and the Founder of CogniCraft Solutions. I am delighted to introduce you to my latest work, "Promise to Wait." Writing has been my enduring passion, and I've invested my heart and soul into this book. It's been a transformative journey, and I am thankful for every step of it.

While pursuing my career in engineering, I've had the privilege of founding CogniCraft Solutions, where I explore and implement innovative solutions. Beyond my professional endeavors, writing has been a constant in my life. This book, in particular, reflects my deep exploration into the themes of life, love, and philosophy.

I have been fortunate to receive recognition for my previous works, including my books "**Life Echoes**" and "**Self Help**" as well as contributions to academia through research papers. However, my greatest joy stems from my connections with readers like you. Your support and encouragement along with my family and friends have been the driving force behind my creative endeavors.

I'm excited to share this latest chapter of my writing journey with you. "**Promise to Wait**" is not just a book; it's a collection of thoughts, emotions, and reflections I hope will resonate with you. Thank you for being a part of this journey, and I look forward to the shared experience of exploring the promises and possibilities of life together.

Warm regards,

Manmohan Mishra

www.ingramcontent.com/pod-product-compliance
Lightning Source LLC
LaVergne TN
LVHW041230150826
845673LV00008B/2340

* 9 7 9 8 8 9 6 3 2 6 3 9 7 *